USBORNE
THE GREAT PREHISTORIC SEARCH

Jane Bingham

Designed by Susie McCaffrey
Illustrated by Ian Jackson

Edited by Felicity Brooks

Scientific consultant: Professor Michael Benton

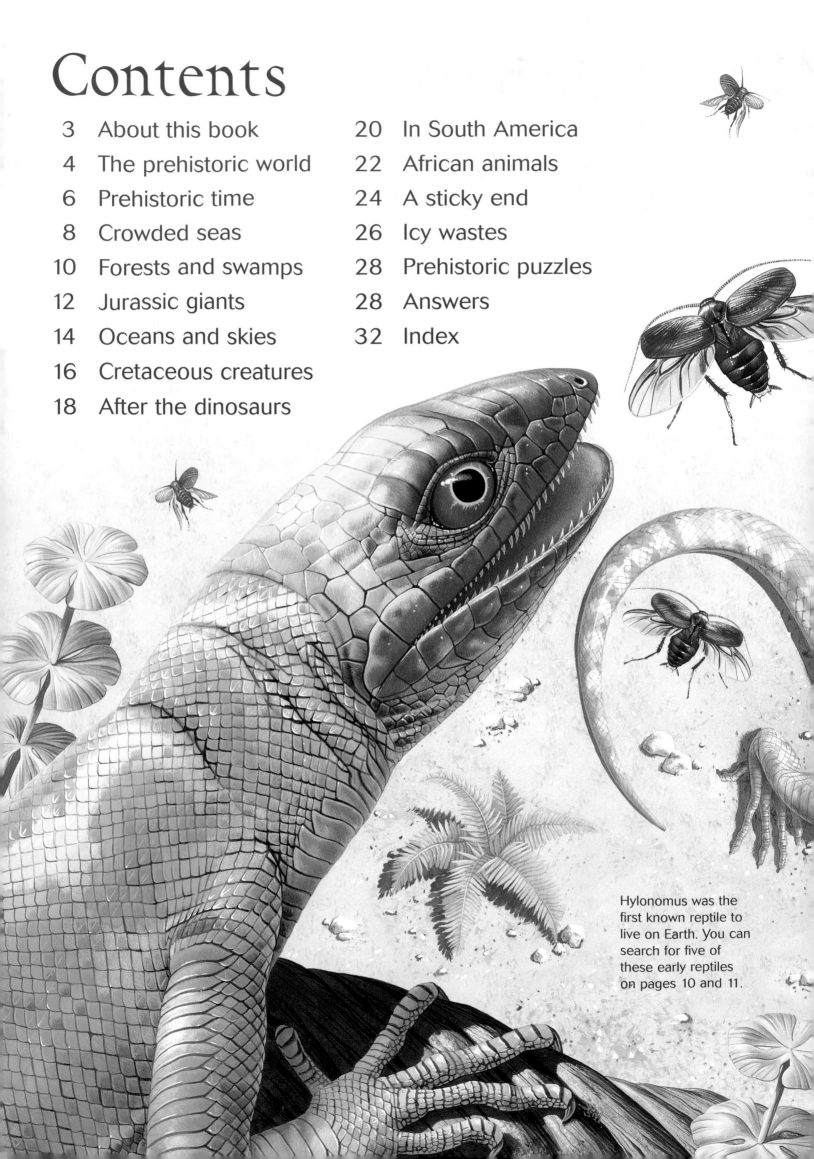

Contents

Hylonomus was the first known reptile to live on Earth. You can search for five of these early reptiles on pages 10 and 11.

About this book

This book is filled with exciting scenes from prehistoric times. You can use it to learn about dinosaurs and other creatures, but it's also a puzzle book. If you look carefully at the pictures, you'll be able to spot hundreds of prehistoric plants and animals. You can see below how the puzzles work.

This strip tells you when the animals in the picture lived.

Around the edge of the big picture are lots of little pictures.

The writing next to each little picture tells you the name of a creature. It also tells you how many creatures you can find in the big picture.

Although part of this dinosaur is outside the big picture, you should still count it.

Sometimes, there are plants and trees to find.

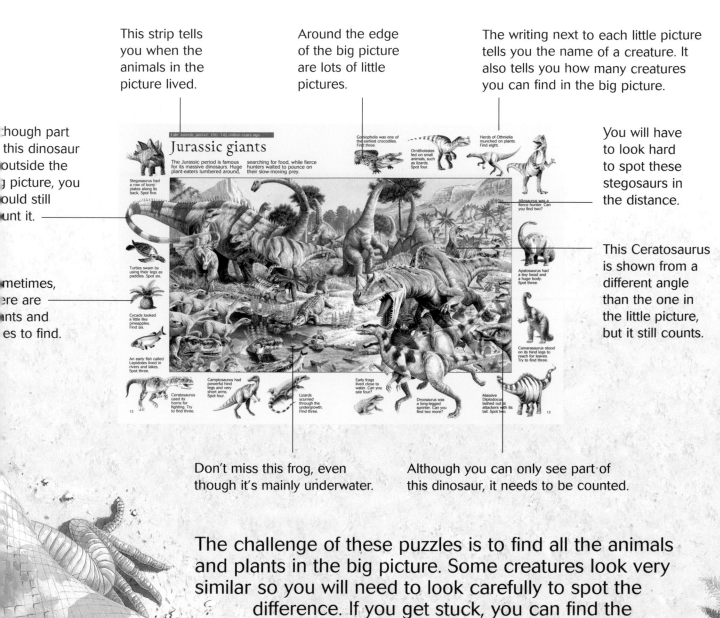

You will have to look hard to spot these stegosaurs in the distance.

This Ceratosaurus is shown from a different angle than the one in the little picture, but it still counts.

Don't miss this frog, even though it's mainly underwater.

Although you can only see part of this dinosaur, it needs to be counted.

The challenge of these puzzles is to find all the animals and plants in the big picture. Some creatures look very similar so you will need to look carefully to spot the difference. If you get stuck, you can find the answers on pages 28 to 31.

To make the puzzles harder, each big picture shows lots of animals and plants very close together. But the prehistoric world wasn't really as crowded as this.

3

The prehistoric world

This book covers many millions of years. Its opening scene is set 545 million years ago, when life was just beginning in the oceans. Later came giant insects, fish and amphibians (creatures that could live on land and in water).

Trilobites were some of the first creatures to live in the oceans.

The first dragonflies were as large as seagulls are today.

This early fish swam in prehistoric swamps.

Frog-like amphibian existed 150 million years ago.

The first creatures to spend all their lives on land were reptiles. They had dry, scaly skin and laid eggs. The larges of all the reptiles were the dinosaurs.

Most dinosaurs were enormous. This foot belongs to a dinosaur that was twice the size of elephants today.

Rhamphorhynchus was a flying reptile that scooped up fish in its beak.

About 65 million years ago, all the dinosaurs died out and a new group of animals spread out across the Earth. These were mammals — animals with fur that fed their babies with milk. Gradually, different types of mammals developed around the world.

The first mammals scampered around under the feet of the dinosaurs. They looked like present-day shrew

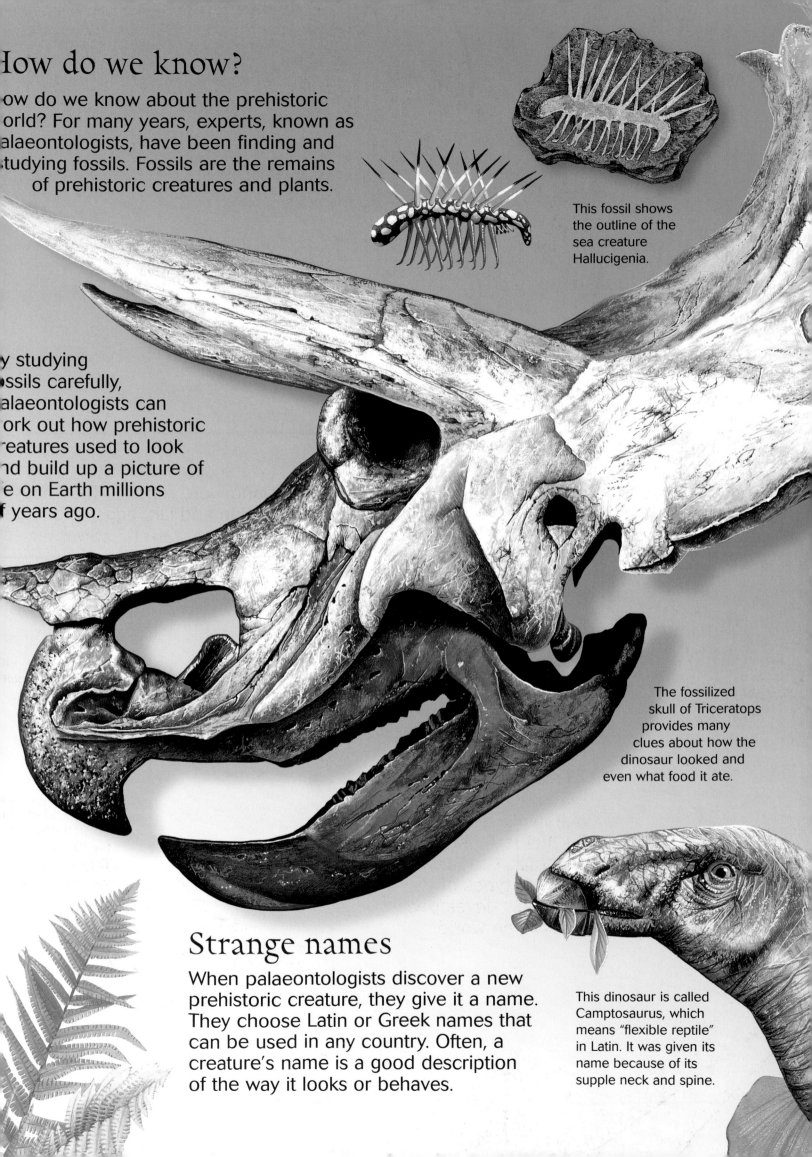

How do we know?

How do we know about the prehistoric world? For many years, experts, known as palaeontologists, have been finding and studying fossils. Fossils are the remains of prehistoric creatures and plants.

This fossil shows the outline of the sea creature Hallucigenia.

By studying fossils carefully, palaeontologists can work out how prehistoric creatures used to look and build up a picture of life on Earth millions of years ago.

The fossilized skull of Triceratops provides many clues about how the dinosaur looked and even what food it ate.

Strange names

When palaeontologists discover a new prehistoric creature, they give it a name. They choose Latin or Greek names that can be used in any country. Often, a creature's name is a good description of the way it looks or behaves.

This dinosaur is called Camptosaurus, which means "flexible reptile" in Latin. It was given its name because of its supple neck and spine.

Prehistoric time

The Earth has existed for billions of years – a length of time so vast it's impossible to imagine. To make it easier to study the Earth's history, experts have divided prehistoric time into different periods. Each period lasted for many millions of years.

This diagram shows the main periods of prehistoric time. You can also see when different animals and plants first appeared on Earth.

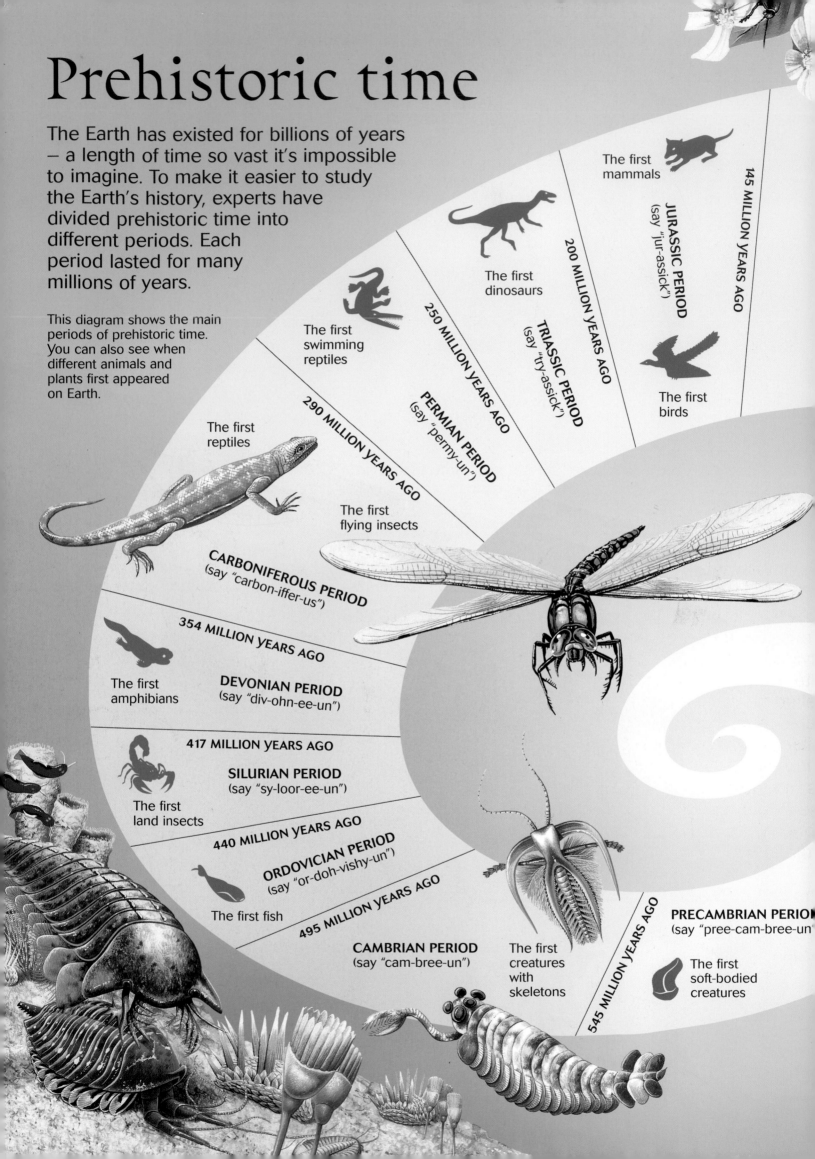

The first mammals

145 MILLION YEARS AGO

JURASSIC PERIOD (say "jur-assick")

The first birds

The first dinosaurs

200 MILLION YEARS AGO

TRIASSIC PERIOD (say "try-assick")

The first swimming reptiles

250 MILLION YEARS AGO

PERMIAN PERIOD (say "permy-un")

The first reptiles

290 MILLION YEARS AGO

The first flying insects

CARBONIFEROUS PERIOD (say "carbon-iffer-us")

354 MILLION YEARS AGO

The first amphibians

DEVONIAN PERIOD (say "div-ohn-ee-un")

417 MILLION YEARS AGO

SILURIAN PERIOD (say "sy-loor-ee-un")

The first land insects

440 MILLION YEARS AGO

ORDOVICIAN PERIOD (say "or-doh-vishy-un")

The first fish

495 MILLION YEARS AGO

CAMBRIAN PERIOD (say "cam-bree-un")

The first creatures with skeletons

545 MILLION YEARS AGO

PRECAMBRIAN PERIOD (say "pree-cam-bree-un")

The first soft-bodied creatures

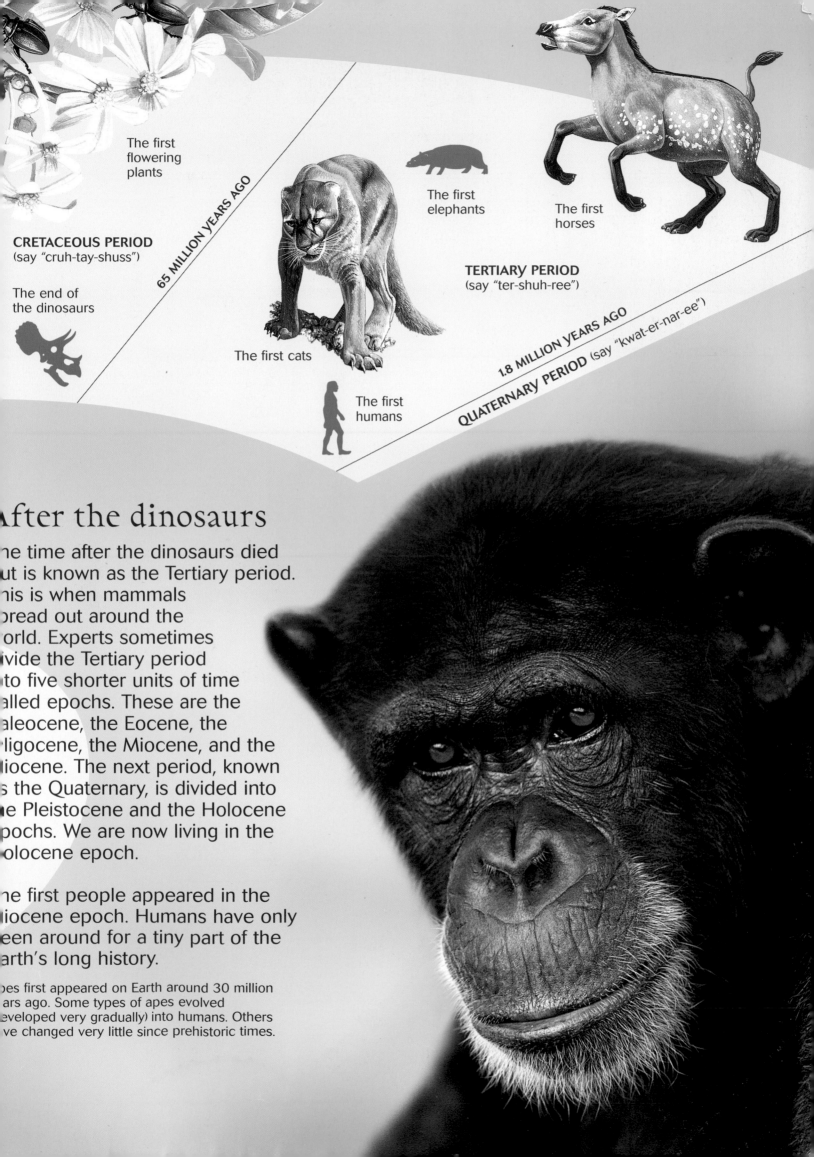

The first
flowering
plants

CRETACEOUS PERIOD
(say "cruh-tay-shuss")

The end of
the dinosaurs

65 MILLION YEARS AGO

The first cats

The first
humans

The first
elephants

The first
horses

TERTIARY PERIOD
(say "ter-shuh-ree")

1.8 MILLION YEARS AGO

QUATERNARY PERIOD (say "kwat-er-nar-ee")

After the dinosaurs

The time after the dinosaurs died
out is known as the Tertiary period.
This is when mammals
spread out around the
world. Experts sometimes
divide the Tertiary period
into five shorter units of time
called epochs. These are the
Paleocene, the Eocene, the
Oligocene, the Miocene, and the
Pliocene. The next period, known
as the Quaternary, is divided into
the Pleistocene and the Holocene
epochs. We are now living in the
Holocene epoch.

The first people appeared in the
Pliocene epoch. Humans have only
been around for a tiny part of the
Earth's long history.

Apes first appeared on Earth around 30 million
years ago. Some types of apes evolved
(developed very gradually) into humans. Others
have changed very little since prehistoric times.

Crowded seas

Around 545 million years ago, an amazing range of creatures began to appear in the oceans. Many of them were protected by shells and spikes. There are 100 creatures for you to find here.

Marrella used its long, wavy feelers to search for food. Find six.

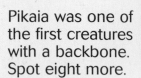

Pikaia was one of the first creatures with a backbone. Spot eight more.

These sponges had long spikes to protect them from hunters. Try finding five.

Transparent jellyfish drifted through the water. Can you spot nine?

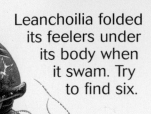

Leanchoilia folded its feelers under its body when it swam. Try to find six.

Odontogriphus swam by arching its body up and down. Spot five.

Sanctacar had 10 claws for crushing it prey. Find fou

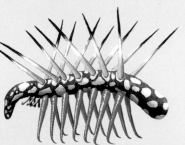

allucigenia
ad two
ws of
ines on
s back.
ot four.

Dinomischus looked like a plant, but it was really an animal. Find 14.

Opabinia had five eyes on stalks and a long nozzle with claws at its tip. Spot three.

Anomalocaris grabbed small creatures in its claws. Can you see one more?

Amiskwia had a flattened body and two small feelers. Spot 10.

Aysheaia had spiky feet for clambering over sponges. Find nine.

ttoia was a rge worm that urrowed into e sea bed. y to spot four.

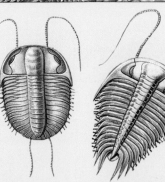

Trilobites scuttled around, searching for food. Find three of each kind.

The shimmering scales of Wiwaxia warned off hunters. Spot six.

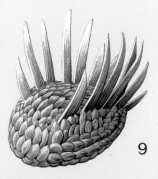

Forests and swamps

During the Carboniferous period, most of the Earth was covered in steamy forests. Giant insects crawled or flew through the forests, and strange water creatures lurked in swamps.

Giant scorpions used their deadly tails to sting their prey. Find four.

Platysomus swam by flicking its body from side to side. Spot 10.

Meganeura was as big as a seagull. Try to find three.

Snake-like Ophiderpeton spent most of its time swimming. Find three.

Arthropleura was a giant millipede that feasted on rotting plants. Spot three.

Cockroaches flew through the air or scuttled over the ground. Find 11.

Eryops looked like a small crocodile. Can you see five?

rly spiders wove simple ebs to trap insects. Find ur spiders.

Centipedes grasped their prey in their fangs. Spot five.

Keraterpeton used its long tail for swimming. Find six.

Tiny leaves sprouted from the stems of giant horsetails. Spot five.

Sigillaria had no branches, just a clump of leaves. Try to find six.

Towering Lepidodendron had a scaly trunks. Spot six.

ylonomus is the earliest own reptile. It spent life on land. pot five.

Diploceraspis had a head shaped like a boomerang. Try to find four.

Tree ferns were plants that looked like palm trees. Try to find three.

Jurassic giants

The Jurassic period is famous for its massive dinosaurs. Huge plant-eaters lumbered around, searching for food, while fierce hunters waited to pounce on their slow-moving prey.

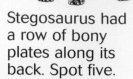

Stegosaurus had a row of bony plates along its back. Spot five.

Turtles swam by using their legs as paddles. Spot six.

Cycads looked a little like pineapples. Find six.

An early fish called Lepidotes lived in rivers and lakes. Spot three.

Ceratosaurus used its horns for fighting. Try to find three.

Camptosaurus had powerful hind legs and very short arms. Spot four.

Lizards scurried through the undergrowth. Find three.

niopholis was one of the rliest crocodiles. Find three.

Ornitholestes fed on small animals, such as lizards. Spot four.

Herds of Othnielia munched on plants. Find eight.

Allosaurus was a fierce hunter. Can you find two?

Apatosaurus had a tiny head and a huge body. Spot three.

Camarasaurus stood on its hind legs to reach for leaves. Try to find three.

rly frogs ed close to ater. Can you e four?

Dryosaurus was a long-legged sprinter. Can you find two more?

Massive Diplodocus lashed out at attackers with its tail. Spot two.

13

Oceans and skies

At the same time as dinosaurs were living on land, enormous reptiles were swimming through the oceans and swooping through the skies. How many flying and swimming reptiles can you find?

Ichthyosaurus looked like a small dolphin. Try to spot five.

Early shrimps drifted through the water. Find six.

Peloneustes snapped up food in its huge jaws. Spot two.

Fast-flying Anurognathus chased after insects. Find six.

Ammonites were protected by a spiral shell. Spot eight more.

Cryptoclidus had long, flexible flippers. Can you see two?

Aspidorhynchus was an early hunting fish. Spot three.

14

Pterodactylus had wings like a bat. Spot three more.

Metriorhynchus was an early crocodile with a tail and flippers. Find three.

Belemnites had long, wavy suckers. Can you see 11?

Muraenosaurus waved its neck around, searching for food. Spot two.

Ophthalmosaurus had huge eyes to help it see underwater. Find three more.

Pholidophorus looked like a herring. Find 18.

Rhamphorhynchus scooped up fish in its beak. Find three.

Scaphognathus used its long tail to help it fly. Spot three.

Giant Liopleurodon was a very fast swimmer. Try finding two.

Cretaceous creatures

This scene shows some of the creatures that lived in Southern England during the early Cretaceous period. At the end of this period, about 65 million years ago, all the dinosaurs died out.

Dragonflies darted through the air. Try to find six.

Pelorosaurus lumbered over the plains. Spot seven.

Hylaeosaurus was covered with knobs and spikes. Find three.

Early seabirds flew overhead. Spot six.

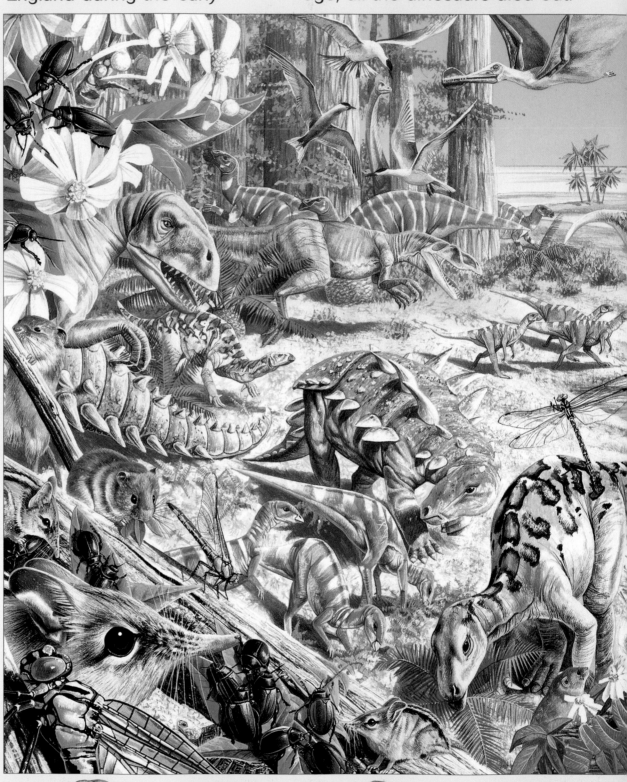

Baryonyx scooped up fish to eat. Find three.

Neovenator was a speedy hunter. Spot two.

Hypsilophodo used its beak to snip at ferns. Find six

Ornithocheirus was a flying reptile with huge, leathery wings. Find four more.

Beetles crawled over leaves. Can you see 14?

Bernissartia was a tiny crocodile. Find five.

Early mammals scurried over the ground. Spot three of each kind.

Pond tortoises lived close to the water. Find six.

Polacanthus was protected by bony plates and spines. Spot four.

Iguanodon had a large spike on its thumb. Spot six more.

...ctisaurus had a ridge along ...back. Can you see three?

After the dinosaurs

After the dinosaurs died out, many new mammals developed. Some were large and lumbering, but others were small and speedy. Climbing mammals lived in trees and early bats flew through the ai

Uintatherium was a massive creature with a very knobbly head. Find two.

Coryphodon loved to splash around in water. Spot four.

Patriofelis looked like a small panther. Can you see three?

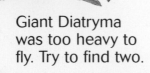

Giant Diatryma was too heavy to fly. Try to find two.

Pristichampsus was a crocodile that lived on land. Spot two.

Stylinodon dug up roots to eat. Find five

Icaronycteris was an early bat. Spot 12 more.

Champsosaurus caught fish in its long jaws. Find three.

Smilodectes could leap from branch to branch. Spot seven more.

Diacodexis was a fast runner. Can you see nine?

Ischyromys climbed trees like a squirrel. Spot three.

Lively Chriacus scampered around, eating insects and fruit. Find four.

Hyrachyus was an ancestor of the rhino. Spot four.

Tiny Hyracotherium was the first horse. Find six more.

Lizards and snakes slithered through the forest. Spot four of each.

19

In South America

Around 150 million years ago, South America became an island. It stayed cut off from the rest of the world for the next 145 million years. Some of its animals were unlike creatures anywhere else.

Peltephilus was covered with bony plates. Try to find two.

Rabbit-like Protypotherium bounded over the grassy plains. Spot five.

Large water snakes waited for their prey. Can you spot three?

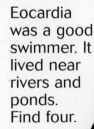

Eocardia was a good swimmer. It lived near rivers and ponds. Find four.

Homalodotherium liked eating leaves. Sometimes it prowled around on all fours. Find two more.

Hapalops often hung upside-dow from tree branches. to find three

omunculus
uld wrap its tail
ound branches.
an you spot six?

Butterflies
flitted
through the
grasslands.
Try finding
17 more.

Necrolestes used
its nose to help
find insects to
eat. Find two.

Astrapotherium
lived on water
plants. Can you
see three?

Graceful
Thoatherium
looked like a
small gazelle.
Try to find nine.

Cladosictis
hunted fish,
reptiles and
mice. Can
you spot six?

Diadiaphorus
looked like a very
small horse. Try
to find nine.

eosodon had
gs like a camel
d a long nose.
an you spot four?

Phorusrhacos
could run fast
but couldn't fly.
Find two.

Borhyaena
had a pouch
like a kangaroo.
Spot two.

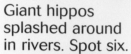

African animals

During the Miocene epoch, some very large animals lived in Africa. Early elephants roamed over the grassland, and hippos and rhinos wallowed in rivers. Can you find 70 African creatures?

Giant hippos splashed around in rivers. Spot six.

Vultures flew overhead, searching for food. Find five more.

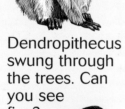

Dendropithecus swung through the trees. Can you see five?

Sivapithecus could stand on its hind legs. Spot six.

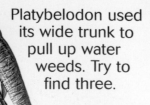

Platybelodon used its wide trunk to pull up water weeds. Try to find three.

Kanuites lived in trees as well as on the ground. Spot five.

Packs of hunting dogs chased after their prey. Find seven.

Teleoceras was an early rhino. Find two.

Aardvarks rooted around for insects to eat. Spot three.

Deinotherium was a giant elephant with downward-curving tusks. Find two.

Prolibytherium had big horns but was actually an early giraffe. Spot six.

Early ostriches could run very fast. Find four.

Tree snakes hung from branches. Spot four.

Afrosmilus was a cunning hunter that could climb trees. Can you spot two?

Hipparion was an early horse. Spot seven.

Percrocuta fed on dead animals. Find four more.

A sticky end

Around 20,000 years ago, many creatures in California drowned in pits of tar. Others came to feed on them, but they became stuck as well. Here are some of the animals that drowned in the pits.

Herds of bison wandered over the grasslands. Can you see 10?

Camelops looked like a modern llama. Spot four.

Teratorns fed on dead and dying animals. Find six.

Western horses were smaller than horses today. Spot eight.

Giant sloths had bony lumps under their skins. Find two.

Weasels raced through the long grass. Spot five.

Eagles swooped down on their prey. Can you see four?

24

rogs and toads
ere trapped in tar.
nd three of each.

og   Toad

Rattlesnakes
could make their
tails vibrate. Try
to spot three.

Smilodon had
huge, curved fangs.
Spot two more.

Dire wolves
hunted in packs.
Can you see six?

Male turkey

Male turkeys had
splendid feathers.
Find three females
and two males.

Female turkey

Storks flew
in to join
the feast.
Find four.

Mammoths
used their tusks
to shovel up
food. Spot six.

25

Icy wastes

During the Earth's long history, there have been several ice ages. At these times, large parts of the globe were covered by ice and snow. This scene is set in Russia during the last ice age.

Megaloceros was the largest deer that has ever lived. Spot three.

Great auks were birds that could swim. Can you see 12?

Arctic foxes were cunning hunters. Find three more.

Lemmings dug tunnels in the snow. Spot seven.

Bears often sheltered inside caves. Find three.

Sea cows had a layer of blubber to keep them warm. Find two.

Woolly rhinos were covered with thick hair. Spot two.

26

hormous whales
unged through
e icy water.
pot two.

Woolly mammoths
had a store of fat
on their heads.
Find five
more.

Seals gave birth to
fluffy white pups.
Find five adults
and four pups.

Arctic hares were
hard to spot
against the snow.
Spot five.

Shaggy musk
oxen roamed
over the snow.
Try to find six.

Reindeer fought
off hunters with
their horns.
Find 11 more.

Arctic stoats could
squeeze through tunnels
after their prey. Spot four.

Elasmotherium
had a huge horn made
from hair. Find one more.

Prehistoric puzzles

Why not test your prehistoric knowledge by trying out these puzzles? You will probably need to look back through the book to find out the answers. If you are really stuck, you can look on page 32.

1. All these dinosaurs except one hunted animals. Spot the plant-eater.

2. One of these creatures is not a bird. Do you know which one it is?

3. Can you guess which of these creatures is not a dinosaur?

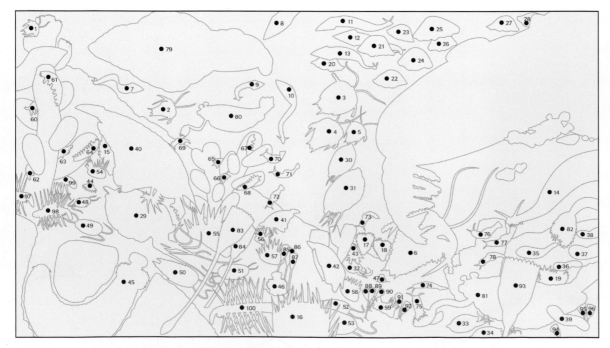

Answers

The keys on the next few pages show you exactly where all the animals and plants appear in the scenes in this book. You can use these keys if you have a problem trying to find a particular creature or plant.

Crowded seas 8–9

Marrella 1 2 3 4 5 6
Pikaia 7 8 9 10 11 12 13 14
Sponges 15 16 17 18 19
Jellyfish 20 21 22 23 24 25 26 27 28
Leanchoilia 29 30 31 32 33 34
Odontogriphus 35 36 37 38 39
Sanctacaris 40 41 42 43
Ottoia 44 45 46 47
Trilobites 48 49 50 51 52 53
Wiwaxia 54 55 56 57 58 59
Aysheaia 60 61 62 63 64 65 66 67 68
Amiskwia 69 70 71 72 73 74 75 76 77 78
Anomalocaris 79
Opabinia 80 81 82

Dinomischus 83 84 85 86 87 88 89 90 91 92 93 94 95 96
Hallucigenia 97 98 99 100

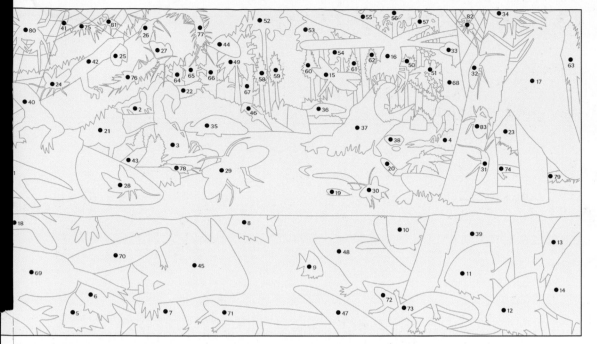

Forests and swamps 10–11

Giant scorpions 1 2 3 4
Platysomus 5 6 7 8 9 10 11 12 13 14
Meganeura 15 16 17
Ophiderpeton 18 19 20
Arthropleura 21 22 23
Cockroaches 24 25 26 27 28 29 30 31 32 33 34
Eryops 35 36 37 38 39
Hylonomus 40 41 42 43 44
Diploceraspis 45 46 47 48
Tree ferns 49 50 51
Lepidodendron 52 53 54 55 56 57
Sigillaria 58 59 60 61 62 63
Giant horsetails 64 65 66 67 68

Keraterpeton 69 70 71 72 73 74
Centipedes 75 76 77 78 79
Spiders 80 81 82 83

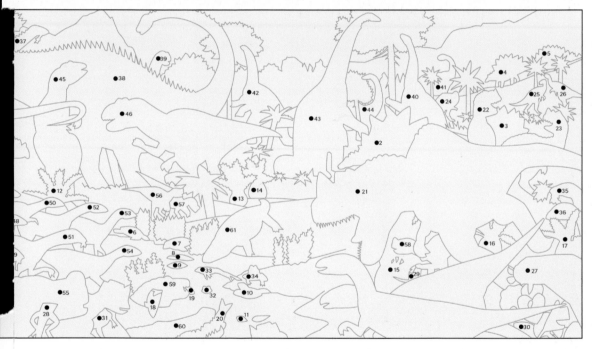

Jurassic giants 12–13

Stegosaurus 1 2 3 4 5
Turtles 6 7 8 9 10 11
Cycads 12 13 14 15 16 17
Lepidotes 18 19 20
Ceratosaurus 21 22 23
Camptosaurus 24 25 26 27
Lizards 28 29 30
Frogs 31 32 33 34
Dryosaurus 35 36
Diplodocus 37 38
Camarasaurus 39 40 41
Apatosaurus 42 43 44
Allosaurus 45 46
Othnielia 47 48 49 50 51 52 53 54
Ornitholestes 55 56 57 58
Goniopholis 59 60 61

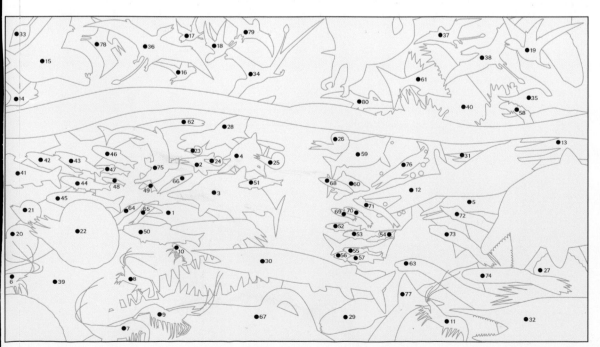

Oceans and skies 14–15

Ichthyosaurus 1 2 3 4 5
Shrimps 6 7 8 9 10 11
Peloneustes 12 13
Anurognathus 14 15 16 17 18 19
Ammonites 20 21 22 23 24 25 26 27
Cryptoclidus 28 29
Aspidorhynchus 30 31 32
Rhamphorhynchus 33 34 35
Scaphognathus 36 37 38
Liopleurodon 39 40
Pholidophorus 41 42 43 44 45 46 47 48 49 50 51 52 53 54 55 56 57 58
Ophthalmosaurus 59 60 61
Muraenosaurus 62 63

Belemnites 64 65 66 67 68 69 70 71 72 73 74
Metriorhynchus 75 76 77
Pterodactylus 78 79 80

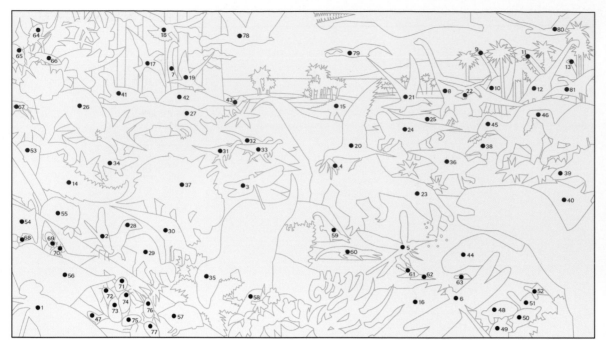

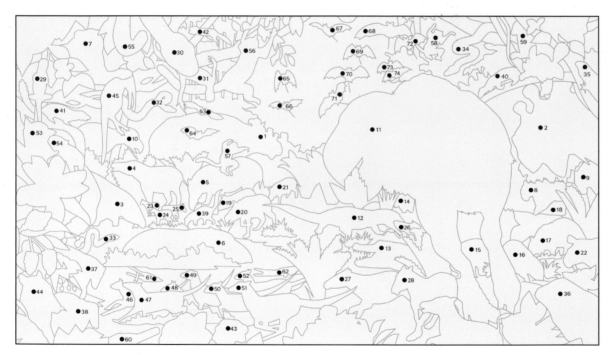

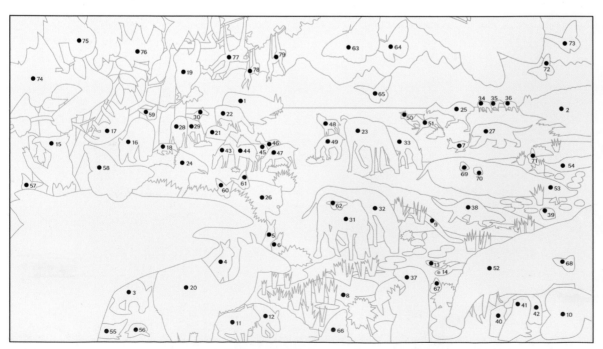

Cretaceous creatures 16–

Dragonflies 1 2 3 4
  5 6
Pelorosaurus 7 8 9
  10 11 12 13
Hylaeosaurus 14
  15 16
Seabirds 17 18 19
  20 21 22
Baryonyx 23 24 25
Neovenator 26 27
Hypsilophodon 28
  29 30 31 32 33
Vectisaurus 34
  35 36
Polacanthus 37 38
  39 40
Iguanodon 41 42
  43 44 45 46
Pond tortoises 47 48
  49 50 51 52
Mammals 53 54 55
  56 57 58
Bernissartia 59 60
  61 62 63
Beetles 64 65 66 67
  68 69 70 71 72
  73 74 75 76 77

Ornithocheirus 78
  79 80 81

After the dinosaurs 18–1

Uintatherium 1 2
Coryphodon 3 4 5 6
Patriofelis 7 8 9
Diatryma 10 11
Pristichampsus 12 13
Stylinodon 14 15 16
  17 18
Hyrachyus 19 20
  21 22
Hyracotherium 23
  24 25 26 27 28
Lizards and snakes
  29 30 31 32 33
  34 35 36
Chriacus 37 38
  39 40
Ischyromys 41
  42 43
Diacodexis 44 45
  46 47 48 49 50
  51 52
Smilodectes 53 54
  55 56 57 58 59
Champsosaurus 60
  61 62
Icaronycteris 63 64
  65 66 67 68 69
  70 71 72 73 74

In South America 20–21

Peltephilus 1 2
Protypotherium 3 4
  5 6 7
Water snakes 8 9 10
Eocardia 11 12 13 14
Homalodotherium
  15 16
Hapalops 17 18 19
Theosodon 20 21
  22 23
Phorusrhacos 24 25
Borhyaena 26 27
Diadiaphorus 28 29
  30 31 32 33 34
  35 36
Cladosictis 37 38 39
  40 41 42
Thoatherium 43 44
  45 46 47 48 49
  50 51
Astrapotherium 52
  53 54
Necrolestes 55 56
Butterflies 57 58 59
  60 61 62 63 64
  65 66 67 68 69
  70 71 72 73
Homunculus 74 75
  76 77 78 79

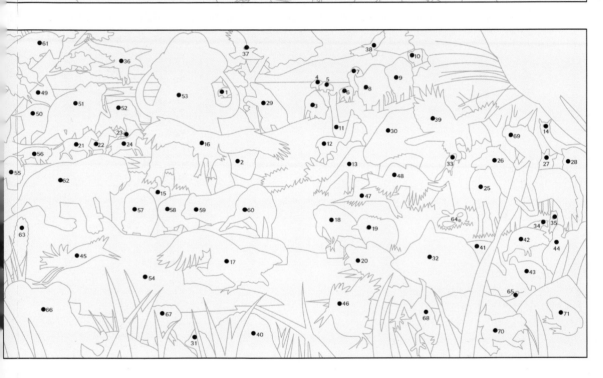

African animals 22–23

Hippos 1 2 3 4
  5 6
Vultures 7 8 9 10 11
Dendropithecus 12
  13 14 15 16
Sivapithecus 17 18
  19 20 21 22
Platybelodon 23
  24 25
Kanuites 26 27 28
  29 30
Hunting dogs 31 32
  33 34 35 36 37
Hipparion 38 39
  40 41 42 43 44
Afrosmilus 45 46
Percrocuta 47 48
  49 50
Tree snakes 51 52
  53 54
Early ostriches 55
  56 57 58
Prolibytherium 59
  60 61 62 63 64
Deinotherium 65 66
Aardvarks 67 68 69
Teleoceras 70 71

A sticky end 24–2[

Bison 1 2 3 4 5 6 7
  8 9 10
Camelops 11 12
  13 14
Teratorns 15 16 17
  18 19 20
Western horses 21
  22 23 24 25 26
  27 28
Giant sloths 29 30
Weasels 31 32 33
  34 35
Eagles 36 37
  38 39
Turkeys 40 41 42
  43 44
Storks 45 46
  47 48
Mammoths 49 50
  51 52 53 54
Dire wolves 55 56
  57 58 59 60
Smilodon 61 62
Rattlesnakes 63
  64 65
Frogs and toads 66
  67 68 69 70 71

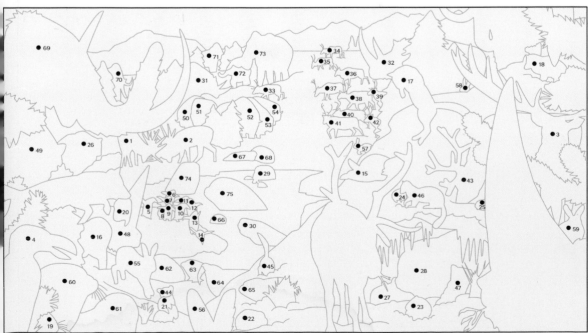

Icy wastes 26–27

Megaloceros 1 2 3
Great auks 4 5 6 7
  8 9 10 11 12 13
  14 15
Arctic foxes 16
  17 18
Lemmings 19 20
  21 22 23 24 25
Bears 26 27 28
Sea cows 29 30
Woolly rhinos 31 32
Reindeer 33 34 35
  36 37 38 39 40
  41 42 43
Arctic stoats 44 45
  46 47
Elasmotherium 48
Musk oxen 49 50 51
  52 53 54
Arctic hares 55 56
  57 58 59
Seals 60 61 62 63
  64 65 66 67 68
Woolly mammoths
  69 70 71 72 73
Whales 74 75

Index

Cover design by Matt Durber • Additional design by Stephanie Jones
Additional editing by Claire Masset • Additional illustration: Inklink Firenze

Picture credit: p7, ©Digital Vision

Answers to prehistoric puzzles: 1. D Camarasaurus, 2. B Anurognathus, 3. D Peloneustes